FROM BERLIN TO HEAVEN

From Berlin to Heaven

Carol Rumens

Chatto & Windus
LONDON

Published in 1989 by
Chatto & Windus Ltd
30 Bedford Square
London WC1B 3SG

A CIP catalogue record for this book is available from the British Library.

ISBN 0 7011 3524 7

Phototypeset by Rowland Phototypesetting Ltd.,
Bury St Edmunds, Suffolk.
Printed in Great Britain by Redwood Burn Ltd.,
Trowbridge, Wiltshire.

Acknowledgements are due to the editors of the following publications:
Aquarius; *Bell's Court*; *Graham Review*, U.S.A.; *Honest Ulsterman*; *Inprint*; *The Northern Echo*; *Oxford Magazine*; *Poetry Book Society Supplement*, 1988, ed. David Constantine; *Soho Square Anthology*, 1989, ed. Ian Hamilton; *TLS*. No. 6 in the sequence, *A Meeting of Innocents*, was commissioned by Birthright, and first published in the Birthright Exhibition Catalogue, 1988.

Some of the poems were written while holding a Northern Arts Literary Fellowship and I would like to thank Northern Arts and the Universities of Durham and Newcastle for their support. I would also like to thank 'British Friends of Israel', who generously enabled me to visit that country for six weeks in 1985.

Notes
'Wealth', p. 26. Rovaniemi: the town in Lapland in which Santa Claus's workshop may be found.
'Jarrow', p. 32. Bede, founder of the monastery at Jarrow, quotes in his *Ecclesiastical History of the English People* the words of one of King Edwin's chiefs, comparing the life of a man to the flight of a sparrow through the firelit hall on a winter night. The 'union-man' is William Jobling, a miners' leader falsely accused of the murder of a local magistrate.

FROM BERLIN TO HEAVEN

PART THREE

PART FOUR

FABLES

PART ONE

From Berlin to Heaven

1 Long Weekend

Wasn't it called the 'Arosa'
– With a whiff of the kitsch South,
A touch of the cuckoo-clock –
Somewhere in the design?
The shutters, painted black,
Though not for some time,
Stood prettily ajar.
Geraniums bubbled over
The flaking sills –
But why was the terrace bar
Permanently closed?
Night after night the chairs
Leaned their hot foreheads
Against the tables.
Songs and laughter rippled
From the other hotels.
Why such silence, afloat
In the city without bedtimes?

We had a last resort
– An inexhaustible
Fridge that shuddered
At its own miracle.
Rows of sleepy bottles
Pointed like little guns.
– Whenever we opened it
They wanted us.
You gave yourself up to a beer.

Mine was something darker,
Oily as plumskins.
I thought of Anna Karenina,
Displaced for love,
And that love died
For want of place,
Whatever was done behind
A gilded room-number
With the passion of grand opera.
Could anything happen next?
The sun was going down
So we let it in,
Small, shy and naked,
And watched the afternoon
Turn pale with marriage.

We ride into our sunset,
Anonymous as exhaust,
Or a chainstore nightie,
Its wishful furbelows
Crushed, forgotten
Under the feather pillow
That won't be mine again.
But the postcards fly
In hot pursuit of us
– The borscht, so red
It ought not to be eaten;
A waiter who speaks Russian
Macedonian-style;
His following eyes,
Jealous as mine will be
When, drunk, you call him
Your brother Slav;
The flatly urban
Subjects you photograph
For sending home:

A used-car sale,
A hedge of scaffolding,
An entrance to the U-Bahn.
So what was there to see
At the border zone?
The defeated foliage?
The unimpressive watch-tower
Anyone could climb?
I lean from the platform
Trying to discover
From a gutted tenement
How you used to live
While you read a guidebook
In one of the mobile toilets
And occasionally groan.

Here I should modulate
To a distant key,
Surprise the hidden, grey
Sweetness of Unter den Linden,
Satirise the two
Basilisks that stamp
Around the Gate.
There is a tour, of course,
But no earthly train
Driving into the iron
Teeth of that river
With the practised whoop
Of a border cavalier,
Could tear from it a promise
To give you back,
And I'm afraid
Some treacherous loneliness
Would wake in each of us
Were I to claim my privilege
And leave without you.

I take your hand instead
And in the spoiling air
Of mythic decay
Still breathed as liberty,
Still bought with blood,
We enter ritual
Like honeymooners
Swaying East
To watch the dawn break
Over Torremolinos,
Or Muslims, slumped
On any dunghill
At the first wail of prayer.
It might indeed have been
Simply a wall
– Some usual, useless,
Surly, inner-city
Lump of municipal shit
The young had tried to claim.
I read the slogans,
The painted names.
Now all I remember
Is 'We have smoked here',
The crimson Cyrillic
Rising clear out of all
That artful, artless writing
On our side of it.

2 *Munich*

Utopia – nowhere
I ever knew
Until that morning.
We had left the sleeper
Blackly streaming
South like an *anschluss*,
A riderless nightmare.
I was still wishing
Vienna, Vienna,
As her breath touched me.
She was pure city
And her brightening forth
In the moment between
Waking and blinking
The heavy gold-dust
Out of my surmise
Was familiar as only
A constant hope is.
We called her 'München',
Tender with surprise.

A sixties child
In a fire-touched brocade,
She curtseyed across
The Marian sky.
If she had willed
Her forgetfulness,
We couldn't blame her.
We too were wide-eyed,
We too, faintly poisoned.
As the day withdrew,
She possessed us differently.

Her shadow found you
And the catch in her voice
Was the buried grace note
Of the Slav.
She turned and turned
Her Russian face
And I heard her whisper
– Extinguishing, enchanting –
Of divorce and marriage
It is divorce
Cuts the deeper heartline:
There can be no future
That is not his past.

Bound to this course,
One night we sat
In futurist Odeonplatz.
Islanded, water-dazzled
Lorelei,
We softly murdered
A *song of the people.*
Our thin strophes
Were the circles where
A mail-coach butterflied
With its snow-faced driver.
As the storm encrystalled
His upturned room
And kneeling horses
To the arched, brilliant silence
Of a polar tomb,
He dreamed a letter home
And his blood-sugar, sinking
Slowly to zero,

Saw him through
To the death-drowsy, solemn,
Last 'I kiss you'.

Perhaps the blur, stinging
Our eyes, was him.
Beyond us, too,
Lay distances,
Blanked by longing,
And, beyond these,
Expectantly
Fading towards us,
The radiance of footprints
We had each called 'family',
And betrayed.
And then I thought
Of a place too small
Even to spell,
A broken star
Where the map creased.
It blazed in the glare
Of an island's crime
Against her continent.
But we went on singing
Until history fell
In easy shadows
At the city's feet
And *peace in our time*,
Our breath said, peace
In our time.

3 Democracy at the Burgerbraukeller, 1926, 1984

We just walked in
And found the moment where
Enormous amber waves
Run beautifully over
The map of soiled empties
And history's remade.
Apprentice Hitler
Jumps on a table,
Trenchcoat-belt frisking
Like a clawed, clumsy tail.
He shoots the ceiling
– A Michelangelo
From the heavy suburbs
Where art is caricature.
Stage dandruff sifts
Onto uniforms, suits.
The patrons still don't know
Whether salvation dances
In such smeared boots.
They study surfaces
Especially those that wink
And brim their glasses
– Worth ninety marks a sip.
When the order comes
To carry on drinking,
Up go a thousand suns.
The chairs scratch and clap
The floorboards' backs,
And full throats roar
How they will always be
For hops and barley
Whoever's yelling 'Time'

At the pantheon
From below an aproned lip.
He shrinks a little now.
He's almost Chaplinesque
But not incredible
(And not quite charmless)
– His glance could quickly pierce
Us where we sit.

4 *Rheinland City Crimes*

There was a youth curled up
On the balcony below ours
One morning.
A scarlet thread
Ran from the resting side
Of the light-haired skull
To the small, exactly-placed
(As it would prove to be) drain.
Neighbours slid from their doors
And took to the public landings,
Darting their eyes to show how
A contretemps had occurred
In the early hours.
The widow had since disappeared
On brassy stilettos
And a puff of Eau de Cologne.

Some dangerous precedent
Had been let loose,
We all knew it,
And, as the morning brightened,
I knew it wanted me.

I waited for it to phone.
Already I could hear
The urgent clicking, through
The wall of atmosphere,
The banked-up heats.
No bell shrilled. But I saw
Its breath condense
In blackmailer's dew
On the grid of the earpiece.

After scrubbing everything
I set off for Holland,
Pedalled flat out
By the unswerving river
That could swallow me and not tell.
I ran into a gatepost,
Thinking about death,
And in my nostrils travelled
The iron smell of blood,
However many bridges
Opened their wings to me,
Flew close, flew past.

I'd known false love could kill
– Could true love, too?
Confused now, I turn
Through the lilac rush-hour.
I think I know what I am.
It is unavoidable.
I shall wait for my victim
Outside where the ghost-shirts
Waft pheronomes not his,
And are his enemies,
My weapon six tired words:
I can't go back to you.

But as I plunge it home
The wrong heart will be there
And I will be alone.
I shall sit out the night,
Tense as a filled glass,
Noticing distantly
That someone or other's tears
Have again lacquered the stars
In the narrow reclamation
Of muscatel city-sky
Where tortured balconies
Try to step upwards, fly.

5 *David*

His home was in Tel Aviv
But he didn't mind Berlin.
Some leisurely Department
Of Guilt, perhaps, or Cleansing,
Had lately appointed him
Writer in Residence.
He wasn't writing.
He showed us, instead,
The new water-colours,
Rainy, soft, Northern.
His poems had translated
To something brighter-lit.

Though we never quite said
The words he wished to hear
He treated us for dinner
At the Grosse Mauer.

Service was ponderous
As a Brahms adagio
Carved with a chopstick
In Chinese granite.
We sat like our starched napkins
– You, depressed and shy
Because you thought us closer
Than was the case:
– We, platitudinous
In the scoured E F L
We felt we had to use,
Both far too courteous
To meet. To live.
He wrote in Hebrew, dreamed
(He said) in Yiddish,
Got by in German,
Remembered Polish.
But now he was worn out
And best at silence.
He feared the path of words
In any forest.
Too many branches threw
Deranging darkness there.

The other day I found
An early book of his,
Opened it at this:
When they call my name
With a Slav accent
It's as if my mother were calling me
To the Sabbath meal.
And I stood still,
Dismayed that we had missed
Something so simple,
Needing only your voice

At its most artless
To tender and release
The familiar shadow,
Spread it at his feet,
Pale with the bloom of snow.
First he would pause and then
See the window change,
The moving, dark mass,
Sheened by candle-light,
Turning into a face
– young, unmarked, long-dead –
That laughed, that let him in.

6 *Jerusalem*

From our window on the third floor
We look down through glass
Into the wakeful restaurant,
Its roof thinly strewn
With rushes, soldier dolls
Pressing their olive knees
Together under the tables.
The tables streaming outwards,
Meeting the competition,
Dissolving in it.
So God diversifies
Into many fields
And some are bloodless.
He can be worshipped here
By sitting stunned and bright
As a shekel in the glare
Of the rival videos.

Their howling close-ups swim
The blue desert night,
Box-office Ayatollahs
Irresistible as sex
And disappointment.

But they are not our drama.
I move from the window
To see how far you've travelled,
To touch the thread
That drew you tense and sinking
Into the clotted weave
Of snow, birch-forest, blood,
And, severed, drifts you back
To your first estranging.
We've slouched, letting our fingers
Creep in each other's pockets
On the Via Dolorosa,
And drunk pure alcohol,
Obtainable all over Zion
From any mirage.
Perhaps that's why you seem
So far from me, so small.
Above the double bed
The air shakes violently,
Becoming water.
As the fan turns its face
First to one, then to the other,
I ask for the last time
The impure but essential question
'Who did you love the most?'
And this is Jerusalem
And so you have to answer
And so the word is made flesh
That will stare at us all summer.

7 Masada

There was one god
Too huge to bury.
We crawl in his frown.
Its lumps and pleats
Ache against
A small, cruel sun.
If sacrifice
Is necessity
And we honour those
Whose blood was teased out
Like a tress of crimson
River from rock,
Should we admire
A truck or plane
That assumes the form
Of a burning bush?

Our cable-car
Shivers, sinks.
Better to say
We're in god's hands
Though his fingers are nothing
But wings and prayers.
We're looking down
On an aftermath:
The sleepy lips
Of the dunes parting
Over steel thumbs:
Transfiguration's
Eye-blink, then
An ash of visions
Where the sky touched Gehenna,

Where we were human
For the last time.

The earth is sweet
But a tar path
Sends us in scalded
Leaps to the sea
And that grainy chair
Is comfortless
As Jordan's arm
Round Israel's shoulder.
Seraphim walk,
Piercing, careless,
All over us.
We hang and hear
The tablets gasp
As a flung bottle
Bursts with commandments:
To be soul
To be salt
To be sky
To be skin
– To be stripped of it.

8 *Religion*

Most days you strolled
The piazzas in shorts,
Baring your knees
Like rosy scarabs
To ward off the Church.
I'd look for the door.

You'd sun yourself
Of find a bar.
I began to get curt,
Felt it a crucial
Impediment,
When carefully you missed
The Maria Assunta.

She rose in her dimmed lamé
Above Torcello
As if she tiptoed
With a mute but piercing cry,
Uncivic, eternal,
On the ashen rim
That was once the world.
You'd have known by what blades
She had been cut
From the craftsmen's hearts
(*And after this our exile*)
– How the tears became dryness,
How the mind shone,
And how the child's weight
Can never be put down.

As for the pantheon
Of the swarming mainland
– Perhaps you were right:
Faith had clutched so warmly
The inscriptive hand,
It died before it knew
And rose as cliché.
I too asked where
The Inquisitor stood
In all this
And saw the air

In canvassed chancels
Dull with used blood.

We sought asylum then
In decomposition.
Refused all icons,
Lapsed. A charred pizza
Smelt somehow of kindness.
Religion was simply
Corn-coloured masses
Of hand-cemented stone,
Flaking into shifty
Waterlights, sunlights
And dust that unremembered
Women swept
And men trod home.

9 *The Stars, or a Tree on Rhodes*

Perhaps we like the myths
Because they rarely claim
To be authentic:
They are simply rooms
To play *perhaps* in. Take
The myth of Helen and Paris.
There are three possibilities.
One, she was seduced.
Two, she seduced him.
Three, only her form
Ran off with him anyway,
Leaving her soul at home
To embarrass Menelaus

Who had no idea what to do
In bed with a woman's soul.
On these three Helens, two
Are caked in a fine dust
Of masculine prejudice.
Seduced, divided Helen
Is Anywoman, lost.
The bright, grape-bunch curls,
Slant eyes, brown waist,
Fade into wispy shorthand
As a jar full of sorrows,
Hunching its shoulders, stares
Deep down into itself,
Into the pores of tradition.
The Helen that remains
Is less negotiable.
She perfumed her wrists
But didn't forget to squeeze
The poisoned tamp against
Her swimming cervix.
Diving between the teeth
Of her beautiful stranger,
She mothered a war
And launched herself.
As Sappho reminded us,
She forgot about everyone,
That most believable Helen
— Even her own children.
So what shall we do with her
Now the jar's alive,
The fire bursting out of the clay
And sprouting into tears?
She's ripe for one last legend
— To be hung with the Dioscuri
Among the brightest stars,

Or hounded out of Sparta
And simply hanged
– According to which Helen,
Which moral, you prefer.

10　*Playing Statues*

Guiltlessly loitering
On what may well be the site
Of a future excavation
– Easy to date
By the pale, immortal,
Wave-buckled bleach-bottle,
And the shadow that was us –
It's good to face south,
An ice-age drizzling
To bronze in the tumbler
With its ghost-kiss of a mouth
From the age of refrigeration.
A roof is vital for this
– One, perhaps, which hums
With beetle-work
And a young vine's distillation
In radiant leaves and topplings
Of cloudless, skin-tight bubbles.
It must be knitted well
With shady minuses
To cool a skull too thinly
Served for its own yolk.
Then, after the blandishments
Of the zinc-top table,
The Asian jig, jangled
On a microchip's pinhead,

And the last, clean rock-fall,
There must be sea.
Superlative exile
From star-nests more remote
Than Copernicus,
Teasing the absolute
We wish on her,
She dissembles mildly
As a picnic cloth, stained
By immortal feasting,
With deeps and wind-plains
Of every conceivable turquoise.
From such a posting,
Hallucinatory
Beyond the captioned glow
We first reclined in,
We can detect the sun
At his daily confidence trick,
The elegant, coasting
Style that suggests progress
But is closer to suspension
– Busy, myopic
As any firing mind.
In the tangible sphere
Long thought inferior,
Earth's patient wash-day,
Hand over hand beneath
The hilly froth,
Is visibly everything
We're boiling down to
– With diminishing hope.
Zephyrs and Vespas,
Winking on the tongue
Of wine-dark bitumen
Waspishly ape

That losable art of horizons.
They surge and drown
In Procrustean silences.
The corpses too,
Chalky or rosy, matt
Or gloss, are mere burlesque,
A miniature send-up
Of high catastrophe.
They lay themselves out,
Thieved pinches of ozone
Scenting the orifices
Where, as the heart stills,
Life, with any luck,
Will open again
Its friendly, crawling eyes
In diamond multiples.
Though light's their element,
These simpler retinas
Are hooded now
With the horrible, peeled blindness
Of statues, approached
Too closely in peopled rooms.
But imagine how
Richly millennial
The stone imagination!
Ours is no different.
Peep-holes compressed
To their shivering fringes,
It gorges on blackness
And dappled fire-squalls,
While a beq more radiation
Than flesh can bear
Frisks the astonished cells
Of a naked marble breast.

11 *Hypothesis*

In Heaven, it's said, we meet
Our relatives. And so,
Love being the thickest, brightest
Of all the body fluids,
I must look forward to
My three handshakes with his past.
Leaving him ungreeted,
We'll take a step closer
To hold each other at arm's-length,
Utter the names we fear.
We'll add the dates and places
Of each attachment, sworn
To keep beyond time and place.
There will be competition
At first, manoeuvres.
But slowly we'll learn
How innocent we are.
Heaven has to exist
If only for people like us
– Haunted, ambiguous,
A veiled colony,
A broken sisterhood.
It is our one chance
To read beyond his eyes
From the mixed grain of our hair,
From the tiny stars of our skin,
To our complicity.
We shall launder our differences
In the strong river of tears
Whose end is sunlight.
And I shall let him go
To each one as she was

In all her young desire
When I was less to him
Than London on the blue
Globe he revolved
With slow-burning fingers
Away from the known world.

PART TWO

Our Early Days in Graveldene

Houses eat money, even council houses.
Ours was officially a *maisonette*.
It was first in a block of twelve, its shiplap coat
Still neat and almost white. We were 49.
Not far from a box of a pub, The Bunker's Knob

– Named for some veteran's clopping wooden leg.
Each cul-de-sac spoke rustic legends: Foxwood,
Broombank, The Grove. I worked on the inside
Where everything could change. I glossed the stairs
Orange. Orange for hope and happy children.

I had two friends in Graveldene, both *Elaines*.
Big Elaine moaned about her hips and her husbands.
As we queued for the bus, she'd shift their weight with
                                                    sighs.
I used to sit in the summer with Little Elaine,
Drinking Coke on her rust-streaked balcony.

She looked too young to have children, and too small.
I was scared sick when her toddler swung the kitten.
He's killing it, I cried. She wasn't bothered.
She smiled with her own kitten-face, creamy, cruel.
I thought of battered babies, I couldn't help it.

There was Stell the single mother, Rose the widow
– Women who worked and were always dashing out
For cod and chips. There was the Rasta, Cyril,
Who slashed his throat that time the bailiffs came.
When they came to us we hid behind the door.

They pushed through a folded paper, promising us
Distraint of Property. Oh boy, we simply
Had to laugh. One mattress, several prams,
A high-chair for the eldest, a rush-mat
Half-way to Shredded Wheat, and the transistor.

'All you need is love', sang the druggy Liverpool voices.
We knew by then they weren't singing for us
And that love ate money, just as houses did.
The sixties were dying, starved for LSD
In the mines and factories, on estates like ours.

We split up in the end. We've done all right.
Sometimes we meet. The other day he said,
'I drove round Graveldene just for a look,
And the door of 49 was off its hinges.
I went inside. I saw your orange stairs.'

Wealth

One Christmas we'd have said 'Rovaniemi'
And bounced in lightly on an Arctic tail-wind
To see the sleigh parked on the airport roof.

I would have steadied you on your first skis
Between the clotted fields, and sent you sailing,
Inarguable brightness overhead,
The clean, etched groove ice-hard in front of you.

Surrey

The birds did not bring leaves
To cover us as we slept
Under the purchased trees;

They were clapping their wings in fear
And we woke to find
We'd abandoned our own children.

We'd walked for a long time.
It was car-drivers' country
And arrival, long-postponed.

So many green vistas
That hugged their fences
– But we tried to appreciate it:

The glamour of leaded lights,
Hedges shady as trust-funds,
As full of rich substance.

A boy stared as he cycled
Languidly down his lane,
Master of every pebble.

We found a bridle-way
Choppy with hoof-prints,
An ungrazed field where

The sweet, high, piercing larksong
Was a burglar alarm
In someone's Mercedes

Parked beyond the stile.
It was a place of signs,
White-lettered threats,

And sometimes less than that
– A skein of wire, strung
Almost self-mockingly,

Biting the leafy dust
Between two rotted posts.
We crossed without noticing

Into the shade-dappled clearing
And knew we'd found just the place
For feasts and happy cries.

From A Geometry Lesson for the Children of England

1 The Triangle

You wanted the cymbals.
  A fat boy got those.

You wanted the side-drum.
  The prefect got that.

You wanted the tambourine.
  A pretty girl got that.

You wanted the maracas.
  A black girl got those.

You wanted to be the conductor.
   You got the triangle.

It's very important to count
   When you've got the triangle.

If you make a mistake
   It sings 'mistake'

In a tiny voice, shameless,
   Above the rest.

The conductor jabs her stick.
   The band lurches on

To the big crescendo.
   Light winks from the silver tubes.

Your chance was trembling towards you
   Why did you forget to count?

2 *A Lesson on the Uses of the Instruments*

What is the protractor?
   A boat no a half of melon
   Says the silly child's pencil

What is the set-square
   A ski-slope whoosh here I go
   Says the silly child's pencil

What is the compass?
   A roundabout just for me
   Says the silly child's pencil

And when you've finished playing
   Says the teacher, snatching the compass
   A bayonet

3 *The Circle*

You choose the dissenting circle
– The one that fits your head
Exactly, and most of your heart.

How comfy to sit in a circle
So nice, your hands ring-a-rosy
With other, like-minded hands.

You chant the high principles
And the quiet rage of your circle
As if they were 'Three Blind Mice'.

Do you know what to sing next?
Do you always know what to sing next
When you sit in the right circle?

4 *More Triangles*

The isosceles triangle
Is lofty and refined
Like our democracy

The scalene triangle
Goes its own sweet way
Like our democracy

The equilateral triangle
Is fair as fair can be
Like our democracy

The obtuse triangle
Seems to have fallen asleep

A Lawn for the English Family

I did not invent this garden
though I put the children in it.
I was not its ruler. I wanted
only pity and beauty to rule it.

Fat dahlias rule it now
and small, flushed fish, strategic
in their twisted pool,
aiming their confidences.

All will be sucked back
into the light one day
and you'll see the eternal law,
the dictatorship of green.

No whisper will shield the rose
in her fevered return to nature,
nor the infant pimpernel
who foresees the weather.

Like an official broadcast
the untaught mouths
of convolvulus spatter white
on tangling wires.

There is a room in the corner
that has crawled out here to die
and the apple-tree hugs its only
apple, its shrivelled soul.

Can you see them at last
swimming the leaves? They are children
who were thrown on the world's mercies,
who were unendurable.

Neither the state nor the state school
nor the solitary jungle-gym
purchased by mail order
could teach them the finished trick

of emergence and escape.
At first, though, they climb quickly.
Their sandals squeak on metal
warm from their hands and the sun.

For a while they can sit in the sky,
laughing at money, its blades
on all sides, slicing and scouring
the shapes of pity and beauty.

Jarrow

Nothing is left to dig, little to make.
Night has engulfed both firelit hall and sparrow.
Wind and car-noise pour across the Slake.

Nothing is left to dig, little to make
A stream of rust where a great ship might grow.
And where a union-man was hung for show
Nothing is left to dig, little to make.
Night has engulfed both firelit hall and sparrow.

Docklands Scenes

Where dirty bonfires
Dream of becoming
Large, clean clouds
And memories are stopped
Like the two stripes of rust
At a vanished gate,
Security fences
Lightly topped
With Docklands Development
Logos, announce
There is life. No death.
Further inland,
Sold and For Sale boards
Clap the sky
Proclaiming how
The City flows
Sweet as the Thames
In a buyer's market.

Somewhere in Bow,
Two men are climbing
The broad steps
Of a newly Sandtexed
Freehold terrace.
With a thin glance back

At the weather-stained
Under Offer sign,
They thump the door
And can hardly wait
To force the lock,
Brutish and slick
As their sucked-in cheeks
And serviceable shoulders.
Rooms dark with mortgage
Hushingly
Permit them to print
The unhoovered carpet.

They move on their toes
Backwards and forwards,
Handling easily
What they knew they'd find
– the gleaming boxes
That wink and purr,
Finger-friendly,
At the heart of success.
But, having soon
Exhausted these,
Each comes out cradling
A chair, the wicker
Sapped and split,
Blond pigtails curling
Stiffly from the seats.
They toss them in the van
And seem content –
Let the yuppie bastards
Sit on the floor.

The van shoves off
With the chairs inside

Weightlessly joshing
The micro trash.
Justice has been done
– By somebody's lights.
The sun is awarding
Stardom to all
The little skipping flags
Of the new marina,
Its idle water
Salmon-skin blue,
And the narrow, high,
Uncleanable windows
Where Ayesha and Soraya
Bend their heads
To the millrace of cotton,
The jiggering needles.

Above Cuckmere Haven

For John Burningham

This is a reachable coast:
The cliff, though it unscrolls
The modest curve of a buttress,
Is no young Atlas
And doesn't presume to try
Shouldering up the sky

– And the sky itself,
Translucent as a harebell,
Pales, but will not disclose
The point at which it wavers,
Becomes an immortelle
Of gases, stars.

The forsaken pillboxes
Doze in their rust,
No patriotic gull
Wooingly calls
The farm-boys to enlist;
Though the air seems prodigal

With ghostly fires again,
These are the grandchildren
Who never went to the Somme,
Dunkerque or Spain,
But packed the silos dumb
With missile-grain.

Visions, like meadow-blues,
Are dust in the hand,
Seed where the grass thins
To light, and where the cliff
Perishes, chalk and sand:
This is a coast of bones.

What remains is a view:
The cliff, upswept from the beach
And the drying threads of the mere,
Lifting whitely two
Crumbling wings, on which
Other wings briefly appear.

Sharing a View

To Leonid Borodin

Stooped in your borrowed
London window,

Look up a little.
Follow the rowan's
Forking paths
To find a thrush
Vermilion-breasted,
Lit like the berries
Whose sprays she twists
And shivers with her need.
Look still higher
– The aerial bracken
Silvers and fades
Till there's only blue,
Wind-washed, familiar.
Call it Siberia;
Pardon these streets
For keeping you.

The First Strokes

Letter to a friend learning English

Before he died, my father drowned in silence.
I thought of him just now, writing to you
In my head about the sea – that medicinal light
I longed to rush to your city of rooms and deadlines,
Your lost July – and it was he who taught me
To swim. In any sea he was stylish, fluent.
He knew its idioms, loved its argument.
So, when my four-year-old, his adventuring grandchild,
Slipped her hold on a wet rock, dropped speechless
Into the swell, he plunged and rescued her.
She used to tell us how huge fish came leering,
Making eyes at her as she bubbled down;

Now what she likes to remember are the hands
That drove apart the soupy green, and calmly
Scattered her suitors, saved her for the sun.
It was soon after this I led him to the pool:
I made him teach me. And, in half an hour,
I had left his side, was lazily at home
In the deepest water, thinking I'd always known how.
It was as simple as doing what he told me
– An obedience I could never risk as a child.
By the time he lost language, I had almost learned
To talk to him. He studied dictionaries
At first with an embarrassed grin, then frowning,
And the deep words we could have plumbed together
Ran white. I thought of all this, writing a blue
Letter about the sea, wanting to coax you
Into the tongue you almost know, but fear,
Having come so late to its stories; wanting to say
That the strokes of an English sentence are easy,
                                        requiring
Only a little self-trust as you kick off
From the margin and glide towards me, sensing all
                                        round you
The solid, patient, unbreakable arm of the water.

After an Emigration

To cut free of the past is not very hard.
You must do it quickly, fall
Absolutely into the offered hand or city.
The past is light, the past is obedient.
It spins from its severed moorings into nowhere.
Only gradually from nowhere it returns.

First it's a dream, at length, a door, open.
Ironical, you appraise
From every angle that city or that person
Not, after all, so bright, free, fascinating
That you were spared the poignant recognitions.
A face floats back. It's yours. You become yourself.

You exist daily on the one thought:
Not that the past was any better than this
But that this is no better than the past.

You try the present again: it isn't yours.

You buy the rounds and abolish past and present.

When the future smiles you edge away: *don't touch*
                                                        me.

Late Travellers

Your antiquarian friend
Shows you a perfect city
On its death-bed of water.

October smoke has stolen
Into the dying hair
Of my lover.

He never touches me now.
The curves of my body do not move him.
There is no language for this.

It weighs on me simply, like exhaustion.

Vair-Me-O

The night, that traditional
Short-cut, where friendly
Differences meet,
Roving instinctively
In the foot-hallowed places,
The air familiar
And dense and fragrant
As they push it gently nearer
Each other's faces,
Is overgrown by sea
And strangeness now,
A permanent travelling tide
Of long black shadows,
Bright-edged and cold,
Where we, with cancelled senses,
Timidly wade,
Not knowing whose lamp, if any,
Stretches its fingers
In hope or in mimicry
Of hope, from the other side.

The March of the Lance-Bombardier and his Children

The road is stopped with corners; darkness moves
All round us like a forest of blue soldiers.
To walk much farther needs a sense of purpose
Beyond the iron love of feet for world.
There are no villages, not a single cottage.
No lights. Yet everybody takes this road.

The mountains have been blinded and let loose
To wander where they like among the planets.
The waterfalls are only storms of ashes,
The loch a vast slate from the tumbled sky.
No headlamps stare, no burning stubs of cat's eyes
– And that's why every driver heads this way.

We turned back for the only certain shelter
(Or so we thought) – the one we'd started out from
In flares of sodium, gassy as champagne,
To plunge into the flute-pure black of pine-trees,
Our torch blanching the rain: yes, we turned back,
While you, with ghostly footsteps – you kept walking.

Was it good, sometimes, to march in uniform
In clouds of human breath between the mountains?
Perhaps it almost felt like solitude
With Ursa Major's posed, angular brilliance
Above your head, more pin-up than Great Bear
And other ranks and stragglers, melting nowhere?

You passed us miles ago, we merely saw you
Vanish. Now you must have turned all corners,
Silenced all waterfalls, and reached at last
The garrison town, to wait for further orders.
Something will happen; something always happens.
You steel yourself for the pitching sea-road: France.

Or else you're only dreaming of it all.
Men can nod off, you said, while on the march.
Their eyes close while their feet, on auto-pilot,
Cleave to the old rhythm of the road.
I didn't ask you if they dreamed as well;
But now I'm sure dreams are inevitable.

You lay your kit out by the barracks window;
You brasso every button till it burns
And waters into stars and leafy sunlight.
You swim the green Ardennes; float back, still sleeping;
Begin to darn your heavy, marching sock.
The needle stumbles brightly, pricks your finger.

Your eyes jump up, salute the road again.
All round you is black Scotland, men and pine-trees
Marching as they breathe. Without agreement
Or argument, they haul the sullen load,
And each turned corner pays out a new length
Of dark. Yet everybody takes this road.

Memorial

I know why you liked marigolds
– They're not afraid of blue.
They drink the sky neat
And toss away the dazzle
Like dogs shaking off a swim.
If you look close you can see
How each slim heart of a petal
Was snipped to the same design.
Their stalks are a rougher breed,
Leaves a thick, oiled salad,
Breath loamy, spiced, not sweet.
I know why you preferred them
To grand blooms gardeners choose.
They flourish on poor soil
And harbour few diseases.
Even at night their closed
Grates keep in a small fire.

They come back year after year.
From the couple of plants you gave me
Sprang this prodigal family,
This garden of lost borders.
It's a place where thoughts of you
Are cut and gilded, sped
On a breeze. The flowers would gladly
Give you themselves if they could
Now, instead of rose-trees
Marching in wintry line
Through a park without children.

Embarrassment

Our parents knew about fear.
What we know is shuffling and lies
And staring down at our feet.
What we know is embarrassment.
And it happens again and again
Whenever we dare to lift
Our glance across Western seas,
We simply can't find our tongues
At the sight of our tired young armies
Who do not know even that.

Reconstruction

The Dietrich Bonhoeffer Kirke
had no name to me then
in nineteen-fifty.
A tall, meat-coloured ruin,

it was perpendicular
but dead-eyed, haemorrhaging
bricks and secret rainbows
in the thickening leafage.
My father told me
it would stand like this forever
to teach the Germans.
As we climbed the wooden bridge
over the railway
I kept looking round
more and more dizzily,
garbling the fact
of cloud with retribution
till a whole fleet glowed there
like cherubim,
each pilot forced to gaze
down through the smoky nimbus
of his last mistake.
Was there truly a pact
between God and ourselves
to hold them eternally
in the sky above Dacres Road
even as they burned
ashen with their planes?
Modest in victory,
I felt their shame, and turned
instead to watch the trains.

White Lego

We have the word Lego
We have the patent the moulds
The plastic. Only the dyes

Are difficult to obtain
In this part of the world.

What we manufacture
Is therefore Building Snow
We truck it in quantities
To our markets cloud-high
Like the top of the volcano

It is on special offer
Because of the rare lack of colour.
It is quite warm to the touch
And unlikely to melt

When your child unwraps it
On Christmas morning say
Immediately Don't cry
You can make a chalkpit
An igloo an ambulance
A cubist polar bear

Your child breathes rapidly
As if to demand
What is white what is Christmas
And you show him just like this

You build and build
Until he smiles
And takes the blocks from you

Don't say What are you making
You know, you are his mother
He is making a garden

It is quite astonishing
Colours are pouring

From his busy hand
Wonderful rare colours
Colours even the rainbow daren't imagine

If when you say to him
One day Look at the rainbow
And he says What rainbow
All I can see is a white curtain
And if one day you pour him
A glass of Cola
And he says My milk tastes funny

He will only be joking

It is good to make jokes
It is good to make gardens
Building Snow makes it possible
For your child to do both

PART THREE

A Meeting Of Innocents: A Birthday Sequence

1 On the bus up the hill
She profiles her best side
With its dangling half-moon.

She wouldn't feel unhip
In Carnaby Street: not really.
Her tights said 'Snow-Flake'.

The fishnet holds her nicely:
Small knees, sharp ankles.
Her jacket's PVC.

Getting off on the hill
She's early for the doctor's.
Nufortes is all there is.

Jukebox, burgers, banter,
Manoeuvres. School's out
– But no-one even sees her.

That's the only fun
Of being eight months gone.
It shows. You don't.

She crams herself between
Chair-and-table, both
Fixed to the floor, rigid

As the laws of fashion are,
But it's O K, she's in,
Leaning on plastic elbows

To kiss the cappuccino,
Forget the doctor's, feel
How it was to be young

Only a minute ago.

2 The rubber flag tightened
And tightened its clammy grip.
Her heart jumped into her arm

And hammered to get out.
She could almost see her blood
Pulsing round faster than lights

On a neon signboard.
Then the soft, easing sag
And another winding up

With a breathless huff-huff-huff
Like the second climax she'd read
She ought to be capable of.

3 She felt good, she felt perfect
But the needle touched the sky.
It said she was four seas over

And still swallowing –
The child, her toxin.
We'll have to induce. She caught

The name: Pitocin.
They took her in, they sent
A girl nurse to shave her

Without a smile but with
A certain cold finesse.
They frowned at the kitten claw-marks

Pimpling her legs,
Gave her a wooden commode
'To spend a penny in'.

She unclasped the earrings slowly
And lay, inert as her tongue
Over the tasteless drug.

It was the usual thing
After all, being too happy,
Being undone.

4 This was how home slipped through unlucky
                                footsteps,
As the solitary cart of belongings
Tilted into the future by itself;

How the sunrise sank in the eye
Of some huge ocean mammal,
Trussed up and drowned on its back

On blazing boards, its mouth
A stretched, horrified vulva.
The comb of filmy tooth

Would be pliable as fingernails
And laced, she thought, with the green
Last meal of a species.

5 She's living in the novel
That was where she learned about birth
And revolution.

She's not the heroine:
Her ankles are tied
Too far, too wide.

She's got muscles, she must try
To grip the subtext.
She grabs some kind of a mike:

This is an outside broadcast,
I'm here, behind the weather,
The frantic jamming.

Eavesdropping, near to tears,
The poetry-writing doctor
imagines what it's like.

To live your life
Is not so easy
As to cross a field.

She thinks of Niagara Falls,
Love's second disappointment.
She could scream: but so many

Acres – and in bare feet –
And the mud churning and shifting –
It's easier to live

Your life than to cross this field.
I'm not just crossing the field. I
Am the bloody field.

6 It was the crying hand
   Thrust from the shawl, unannounced
   As celandines in cold March grass.

   It was the five little swimmers,
   Waxed in each wrinkle and seam,
   Bent at the waist, sea-wearied.

   It was the stronghold they shut
   Round her probing finger, the way
   The crying shivered into stillness,

   That made her think that the teeming
   Shambles of it all was planned,
   And the plan was matchless.

7 They brought her the baby
   Every four hours for precisely
   Five minutes on each breast.

   But the child had travelled too far:
   Its lips worked busily
   Then slowed, slipped open

   In the trance of a lost time-zone.
   She could have waited all day,
   Conversed with it haltingly

   In handfuls of dreamy sucks.
   No lover's mouth was exact
   Like this, no head so neatly

   At rest where her armskin was palest.
   But they lifted the child away
   And frowned over the scales.

She'll cry later on, they threatened.
Such a thin, inaudible, public
Lament, she thought. The lace cones

Of the nursing-bra turned yellow
And crusty with wastage.
Her arm felt cold. The child

Cried on, somewhere. She cried.
She thought: this is where money starts.
This is how candy's made.

8 She discharged herself politely.
Rode the tall white hospital bus
To her mother's house

– A popcorn maisonette,
Its walls bright-speckled,
Its windows glaring.

Her father came in,
Politely drunk. Withdrawn.
He didn't dislike children

But when, in the kitchen,
She began to unbutton her blouse,
He sent her to her room.

She went out, the high street
Made her dizzy.
She sat in the garden

Among the little rocks
While her husband's mince dinner
Dried out on gas mark three,

The white page in her hand,
On which nothing was written,
Translucent with sunlight.

PART FOUR
FABLES

As if a Prayer

For Salman Rushdie

As if one open space were left inside the grain of sand. As if one immaculate desert, one kept rainforest, one indissoluble crystal were left. As if nothing there could be imaginable. As if you crossed the border of yourself and reached the loneliness beyond tears. As if you crossed other borders. As if you laboured. As if freedom.

A real gun, an eye without an imagination, a mouth without a nose for analogy, would thrust a long shadow into that place. Would say God had been offended and it was God's avenger. Would say to you die.

As if God were imaginable other than as the one open space inside the grain of sand.

Inflation

I stand on the edge of the place where I am expected to become invisible. I ask if this is all there is.

The fog lifts slightly and I walk towards an area slowly creasing into water. I look into the water and can just see a blur of grey. I do my hair, combing it carefully over the place where my scalp shines through.

When I look up, a young ferryman is standing in the

shallows. Once, I would have caught him in my arms and pressed his body into mine: I would have fingered obsessively the small curls on the nape of his neck and pretended to read his soul. Now I feel nothing but hatred for him.

He grins mockingly and holds out his hand, making a deep bowl of the palm.

I lie that I have no change, not even two obols. He doesn't understand, or pretends he doesn't. His eyes still mock me.

When I have explained, he says he will not accept foreign coins. He mentions a three-figure sum, and demands a cheque, made out in sterling.

And it turns out he doesn't even go all the way to the underworld.

Queen Bluebeard's Palace

Henna peroxide vitapoint hair gel block powder loose powder avocado neck-cream elberberry eye-cream – you won't catch me out, I'll never go into your prison. I may choose you for pleasure. Never from necessity.

But I still have to climb the stairs and go from room to room, decade to decade.

I peer round each of the doors. The women smile back. They always look young, even in the rooms at the end of the corridor.

But then I come to the last room. I open the door. An old hag frowns at herself in the mirror as she twists the rollers from the colourless, thin strands of her hair. She brushes the frizz out happily. Then she tries different-coloured scarves against her crumpled throat.

And suddenly I'm screaming like a brutally
disappointed child – don't do it, don't say there's
nothing else, why isn't there something else I want
there to be something else

The Guilt Dragon

It is bigger than the Virus Dragon.
It doesn't often kill
But can strangely encumber you.
Some say it has to be faced
Before a scared breast can be unlaced,
Before a girl may know
Even by her fingertips
How strangely malleable
The hardness of her lover is.

Lacunae

Once more the name of the earth she stood on
                        changed.
The pine-tree's name changed.
The pebble's name changed.
The mud's name changed.
She still spoke to them in the oldest language.
A child pointed at her. A uniformed man
Took her arm. She explained
The pine-tree still speaks Pine-Tree,
The pebble, Pebble, the mud, Mud.
She used the old words. The child giggled.

The man tightened his grip, her arm-bone sang
And the mud, the pebbles, the pine-trees
Broke suddenly into unrecognisable pieces
And rushed into her face, and blinded her.

Perestroika

This is my sadness
– To have been the future
You thought you wanted.

This is your sadness
– That the most astonishing future
Began without you.